Transitions

A Guide on Moving From Law Enforcement or the Military into a Second Career

By

Michael V. Maddaloni

ISBN: 1-4033-7985-8 (e-book)
ISBN: 1-4033-7986-6 (Paperback)

This book is printed on acid free paper.

tBooks — rev. 11/15/02

TABLE OF CONTENTS

INTRODUCTION

As we enter the 21st century, there are more people in the public sector than ever before. The challenges presented by a growing population, a smaller world, and our national security have combined to create an increasing number of positions at various levels of government.

While their duties are varied, most public servants share several common characteristics:

- They have never worked in the private sector; if they have, it was only for a short time.

- During their public service careers, they will accumulate considerably less wealth than their private sector counterparts. This is especially true for those with a college education.

- They will retire, with pensions, in their 40's or early 50's and most will seek second careers. These second careers will typically last from ten to twenty years.

- **While most who start second careers will wind up in the private sector, few have a clear concept of how the private sector really operates. This places them**

at an extreme disadvantage as they seek employment and strive to succeed in their new careers.

I have traveled extensively across the country during the past several years to present my one-day seminar **"Transitioning from Law Enforcement to the Private Sector".** During these presentations, and in private conversations with seminar attendees, it became very apparent that the statement made in the last bullet point translates into numerous obstacles for those in transition.

The concerns mentioned to me most frequently include:

- Very little, if any, knowledge of how a typical business operates.
- Problems formulating effective resumes that employers will want to read.
- Lack of knowledge on how to pursue non-published job opportunities, which incidentally, represent about 80% of all jobs available.
- A lack of awareness regarding private sector compensation issues.
- Problems preparing for and handling private sector job interviews.
- Problems with transitioning effectively into a new job and corporate culture, particularly during the first year.

As one who spent many years in both federal law enforcement and the private sector, I have a keen appreciation for the issues encountered by those in transition. In retrospect, I wish that I had been more aware the subjects covered in this book when I made my transition twenty years ago. The preparation of this book, albeit with the benefit of hindsight, was designed to help readers avoid some of the pitfalls and oversights encountered by myself and others

In this book, we will emphasize the issues most relevant to those in transition. The information provided here will hopefully increase your knowledge in key areas and better prepare you for the tasks that lie ahead. The content closely approximates what we cover in our seminar and should serve as a useful reference as you pass through the various phases of transitioning to a second career.

While this book and my seminar are designed primarily for law enforcement and military personnel, it also has considerable applicability for other career civil servants who are planning second careers.

1.   PLANNING A SECOND CAREER

Perhaps the most important element of moving into a second career is to formulate and execute a plan that enables you to assess where you are in your life and takes you where you wish to go.

If you fail to develop a plan, you will often find yourself wasting valuable time as you search for a job. You may also find that the job you wind up in is not really what you were looking for in a second career. These are not minor issues. Finding a job, especially a good job, is time consuming and an emotionally draining experience. It's best that the time frame needed to do this be relatively short (three to six months) rather than over a long period of time. A protracted job search can be very disruptive to your regular routine and may tend to dampen your overall enthusiasm to consistently do what is required to make a job search successful.

In addition, you don't want to wind up in a job that doesn't suit you. This will not only make you unhappy, but may also cause your employer to be dissatisfied with your overall performance. Feedback I have received from seminar attendees and others suggests that a fairly high percentage of public servants leave their first private sector job within two years. This is often due to the lack of developing a career plan before leaving the public sector. So, before you start looking for a job, think about the points covered in this section.

It's never too early to start planning

Too many of us don't really plan a second career until it's almost time to make a change. To an extent, this is human nature because we tend to spend most of our time and energy dealing with current events. The problem with this is that we often find we have not prepared ourselves for the next important phase of our lives. Very often, education, training and other issues needed for success in second careers can easily be addressed well before the second career begins. Obvious examples of this include formal education, second jobs, and even hobbies that can better prepare you to meet the challenges that lie ahead.

Perhaps one of the best examples I have come across is a fellow who was a Sergeant with the Philadelphia Police Dept. He attended one my seminars and I had the opportunity to speak with him when the session was over. I was so impressed with his story that I started using it in my seminars. This man started with the Police Department as a twenty year old with only a high school diploma. At the time I met him, he had seventeen years on the job with three years to go until retirement. Since he started his law enforcement career, this man managed to obtain a Bachelor's degree in Accounting from Temple University. He followed that up with an MBA in Finance. He also managed to obtain a CPA, a real estate license, and a license to sell securities. He worked part time in a business preparing tax returns, selling commercial real estate and developing some clients for his insurance and brokerage business. Eventually, he obtained a partial ownership in the business and finally bought the business outright. He hired people to work in the business while he continued with his law enforcement career. Due to his business interests, he encountered additional opportunities and purchased a sandwich shop, which is now run by his cousin, and later a beauty salon, which his wife manages. At the time I met him, his non-police income from these ventures, *after* operating expenses, was about $150K a year. This is a good bit more than what is earned by the police commissioners of Philadelphia and other major cities. It's also more than what is earned by most people in private sector security jobs.

Is there much doubt that this fellow pretty much has his second career not only planned, but up and running?

While this may represent a rare example of planning a second career, the point here is obvious. You can and should, to the extent possible, gain as much education and experience as you can for your second career while you are still in your first career. This will place you in an excellent position to make a smooth transition when the time arrives.

Remember that if you haven't done anything yet to prepare yourself, it's never too late to start.

What are your choices for a second career?

Obviously, your choices are far too numerous to list here. The most important decision to make is whether you want to stay in the field you are in or make a complete change. Many of us have the urge to make a complete change and then realize our marketability, for the most part, lies in what we have done for many years. Since my Secret Service days, I have always wanted to diversify into things that were different, interesting, and financially rewarding. Over the years, I have found that the best way to do this was on a gradual basis. While my first job after law enforcement was working in security management for a large corporation, I find myself today involved in several different ventures. My security consulting business still represents a significant part of my earned income, but most of the income now comes from other ventures. My eventual goal is to derive all of my income from ventures outside of security consulting. After all, I have been in this business for over thirty years. That's a long time for a person to be in any field.

As you prepare for your next career, your choices essentially lie in three main areas:

- You can obtain another **public sector** job. I know quite a few individuals who retired from the Secret Service and went to work for other agencies in the Federal Government. They are often referred to as "double dippers" because they draw a pension and a paycheck from the same employer. Not a bad idea if you don't mind continuing to work for a government agency. This is generally a very safe career path.

- You can enter the **private sector** and work for a corporation.

- You can become **self-employed.**

What path you choose is very important because it will form a key element of your eventual career change.

It can be difficult to choose which of these three directions is best suited for you. Ultimately, you will have to make the decision based on a number of factors, many of which are based on personal preference, job availability, family considerations and your financial situation.

If you are interested in the opinions of those who share your background, take a look at the following chart. It is the consensus of several hundred opinions provided to me over the past five years by those who moved from the public sector into either self-employment or corporate jobs..

	Corporate Job	Public Sector	Self-employed
Base Salary	Above average	Average	Above average
Bonuses	Average	Below average	Above average
Fringe Benefits	Above average	Below average	Above average
Job Security	Average	Above average	Below average
Job Satisfaction	Average	Below average	Above average

The left column lists what are undoubtedly five key factors most of us would associate with any job. Each person polled was asked to give an opinion regarding whether they thought these factors should be rated as above average, average, or below average in relation to the career path chosen. Some of those polled had worked in all three areas, all had worked in at least two of them. What path you choose will be based on many elements such as tolerance for risk, your financial situation, and what environment you feel the most comfortable in. If you know what area you wish to pursue, you can limit your job search to that area. If you are not sure, you can look for across the board opportunities and evaluate them as they come along.

Conducting a Self-assessment

Another important element of the planning process is to conduct a self-assessment. This will help you evaluate your strengths and weaknesses and perhaps give you some insight into exactly what you should be doing or avoiding in your second career. Many of us have never done a self-assessment, we simply go along year to year doing the same thing without any regard for changes that occur within us as we age, become more experienced, gain more financial security, develop new interests, etc.

Take a look at the chart below. It lists ten factors that should be part of assessing yourself for a second career. There are certainly other factors as well, but for now let's just use the ones listed on the chart.

SELF ASSESSMENT FACTORS

ADAPTABILITY

FLEXIBILITY

WILLINGNESS TO LEARN

CREATIVITY

INDUSTRY CONTACTS

MARKETABILITY

PROFESSIONAL EXPERTISE

ORAL AND WRITING SKILLS

INTERPERSONAL SKILLS

DRIVE AND ENERGY

Grade yourself in each of the categories from 1-10 with 1 the lowest score, 5 average and 10 the highest. **Be honest with yourself,** no one is going to see the results but you. If you are below average in any of these areas, is there anything you can do to improve yourself? Usually there is, but sometimes the answer is no. Many of us, for example, do not have the drive and energy in our 40's and 50's that we had many years ago. If this is the case, admit it to yourself and avoid taking a job that has heavy travel demands and/ or very long hours. If you don't think your oral and writing skills are good, you can do something to improve them. If you are not willing to learn, you can change, but will you? How good is your creativity? If you have never been creative, you probably are not going to start now. Is the knowledge you have of your profession current or outdated? If it is outdated, you should attempt to make improvements as soon as possible.

The bottom line here is that you should be aware of your overall strengths and weaknesses. Improve your weaknesses wherever you can and consider both your strengths and weaknesses as you embark on a second career. If you are especially weak in any of these areas, consider what you can do to improve and try to determine how it may affect your job search and performance. Far better to be aware of these things now than find out about them later. During my business career, I had two subordinates from essentially the same background. One had drive, was eager to learn new things, very flexible and adaptable. He was an extremely valuable asset to the company. The other did just enough to get by; he basically wanted to put in his time and collect a pay check. Both the company and this fellow would have been better off if he had retired out right after his initial career.

Developing a time line- when do you want to make the change?

Another important element of planning is to develop an actual time line for your job search. Many have asked me when they should start looking for a job. For the most part, it depends on when you are in a position to leave the job you are now in. If you need a certain amount of time to become eligible for a pension and you are close to acquiring the requisite time, you probably want to stay in your current position until you become pension eligible. On the other hand, you may be a long way from becoming pension eligible and just want to make a change. If this is the case, there are no time constraints to your job search.

If you do have time constraints to remain in your current position, you should probably not begin your search until you are within six months of being able to make a move. Should you find a job early on, say three months into your search, most employers will wait a few months for you to start a job. Usually, they won't wait too much longer, assuming they need the position filled within a reasonable period of time. You don't want to start a search too soon and then wind up with a job offer you really can't accept because you have not yet become pension eligible. This is a tremendous waste of time and energy and doesn't serve any useful purpose for either you or the employer. I have seen more than a few persons have to pass up good job opportunities because they received an offer too early.

Another factor is whether changing jobs may involve relocating to a different area. Many employers will want you to start a job within a month or two of accepting an offer, even if you have to move. Most will pay for you to live in temporary housing for a limited time. So, if your job search is going to include relocating, you should be sure that you are able to make the move within a relatively short period of time. This may require you to make a move on your own and leave your family behind for a period of time. If you have never gone through a relocation, the process of relocating and starting a new job at the same time can be particularly stressful for you and your family.

If you wish to eventually retire to a particular area, you may wish to search for a job near that location. This has several obvious advantages, but it will narrow the scope of your overall job search.

2. BUSINESS OPERATIONS

Although most will wind up in the private sector for second careers, few understand very much about how the business world operates. This is understandable, because for the most part, most have never worked in a private sector job prior to their public sector careers. If they did, it was more than likely for a relatively short period of time and under much different circumstances than exist today in the business world.

Before embarking on a job search in the private sector, it is important to understand a few things about how a typical business operates. This will provide you with some valuable insights as you look for job opportunities and prepare for interviews. It should also prove useful to you during the first six months to one year on the new job.

Comparing the public and private sectors

Numerous persons who will make the transition to the private sector feel that the two sectors are very different and share few similarities.

13

I don't believe that is the case. While there are differences, the two sectors have much in common. To begin with, both sectors are staffed with people who need to work for a living and, for the most part, people tend to be the same no matter where they work. Regardless of what sector you work in, you still have co-workers, you need to interact with others, and you have a job description that describes what you are supposed to accomplish while at work. You also have to deal with bosses, office politics, balancing your job demands with those presented by your private life, and a variety of other issues that vary from person to person.

Having said that, it is important to understand that there are some major differences that one should understand before embarking on a private sector career. The main difference, in my opinion, is that the public sector is designed to be service oriented while the private sector is, by design and necessity, oriented to create **profit.** Companies that don't make a profit can't stay in business which means that their employees wind up out of work. Public agencies, in the main, will continue to function with revenues obtained from taxpayers. While it is true that in some cases tax bases may decrease for a variety of reasons, most public agencies stay open.

Those who enter the private sector must understand that most of what happens in a typical business is done to generate as much profit as possible. In the private sector, your salary represents an expense that reduces the company's bottom line. In order to justify your salary on an ongoing basis, you are going to have to show the company that the cost of employing you is achieving at least one of four objectives:

- You are selling(or making) products or services that generate revenue for the firm
- Your function adds value that enables the firm to operate more successfully
- Your function is required to meet regulatory requirements imposed by the government
- Your function can protect the company from losing revenues

In general, if you can't meet at least one of these criteria, the company has no use for you. That does not mean that they will ever realize it and eliminate your function, however, in today's business environment, dead weight isn't carried very long. Another thing to keep in mind is that just because your function is needed, you are not guaranteed a job. If you are not getting the job done, you are much more likely to lose that job in the private sector than you are in the public sector. The public sector, in general, is more likely to carry average to below average performers due to a combination of civil service regulations and the fact that they do not have to show a profit at the end of each year. The private sector generally will not do this because they can't afford the luxury. Managers in the private sector need to maintain productive subordinates in order to maintain their own jobs, and they are not going to carry someone who doesn't get the job done. It is important to keep this in mind for the entire duration of your private sector career.

Description of major corporate functions

We'll start by taking a look at an organizational chart for a typical large business. You will find these functions in most businesses although the reporting relationships shown below may vary. Following the organizational chart, we will briefly examine the main duties of the various functions within an organization.

Shown below is an organizational chart for senior management. Some firms may have more or less functions, but what is displayed here is fairly typical. They represent the various operating and support functions that most firms need to operate successfully. When you enter the private sector, you will work in one of these functions and possibly provide services to many of the others. It is important to understand what these functions strive to accomplish, how they operate, and what interactions take place between them.

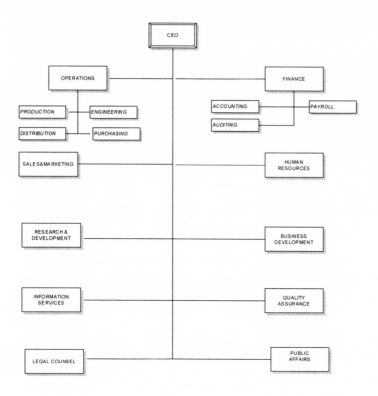

- **CEO or Chief Executive Officer**- The most senior executive in the organization. This position may report to a Board of Directors and will usually have a position on the Board. CEO' s are responsible for all business operations and are the top decision maker in an organization.

- **Operations**- This is a function that is tasked with acquiring raw materials, manufacturing, providing service and shipping products. It typically includes all manufacturing and distribution locations as well as the purchasing and engineering functions.

- **Finance-** This function is responsible for all accounting, auditing and payroll functions within a company. They are responsible for receiving payments, paying bills, preparing financial statements, and conducting necessary financial analysis of the company's business operations.

- **Sales and Marketing-** Is responsible for selling and marketing the company products. Typically, it includes all inside and field sales personnel, as well as employees who have marketing and advertising responsibilities.

- **Human Resources-** This function is responsible for maintaining company policies that deal with personnel issues. It typically includes duties such as recruiting, labor relations, benefits, employee health and personnel administration. It may also be responsible for training, safety and security.

- **Research and Development-** These functions are responsible for developing and bringing to market new products or updated versions of existing products. It takes on an increased importance in industries such as computers, telecommunications, bio-tech, and pharmaceuticals.

- **Business Development-** Is responsible for finding new or expanded business opportunities for the company. It may play a key role in mergers, acquisitions and the forming of alliances or partnerships with other companies.

- **Information Services-** This function is usually responsible for acquiring and maintaining all data processing, communication and internet services utilized within a company. It has taken on an increased importance in the last ten years.

- **Quality Assurance-** This is a function tasked with assuring that the products made by the company meet standards that are consistent with manufacturing specifications and good business practice. They often handle customer product complaints and product recalls.

- **Legal Counsel-** Is responsible for handling all legal matters within an organization and providing various departments with legal advice when needed.

- **Public Affairs-** Is tasked with handling media communications and acting as the voice of the company to the media and public. It may also be responsible for handling company publications such as the annual report and employee newsletters.

Some of these functions such as Research, Operations and Sales are core functions needed for the company to operate day to day. Most of the others are staff functions that provide specialized support to the core functions as well as to other staff functions. Companies must maintain basic core functions to operate, they do not necessarily have to maintain *all* staff functions. During times where companies have to cut expenses, they will usually look to reduce staff functions before they cut into functions that are developing, manufacturing and selling its products. It's best to keep in mind, however, that no job is completely safe.

Factors that impact a business

There are many factors that impact a business, some more than others. As you search for a job and think about joining a particular organization, you should understand how various factors may come into play. Some of the things to consider include:

- **Industry Type**

   Some industries carry more risk than others. As an example, companies that sell consumer staples such as food and drugs usually carry less risk than an internet start up or a travel related business. Often times, the higher risk firms offer higher salaries and incentives.

- **Competition**

   How competitive is the industry that a company operates in? The more competition there is, the harder it will probably be to achieve success on a regular basis.

- **Product Line Maturity.**

Does a company derive a large portion of its revenues from selling off- patent products that have been on the market for a long time? Firms that do often lag behind companies that are innovative and frequently bring to market new or updated products.

- **Global Economy**

The global economy has a direct impact on the success of most organizations. If, for example, a company derives half of its revenues from Asian markets and that part of the world it hit with a long-term recession, the company may suffer a significant shortfall in revenues.

- **Currency Exchange Rates**

The exchange rates for foreign currencies have a direct impact on profitability to the extent that a firm is involved in overseas markets. A firm that realizes a large percentage of revenues from overseas markets may suffer serious consequences if there are adverse fluctuations in the exchange rates between the US Dollar and key foreign currencies.

- **Patents**

Firms that introduce new products typically obtain exclusive patent rights to those products for many years. Companies that are able do this on a regular basis are usually very successful and highly sought after by job applicants.

- **Cyclicality**

Some firms derive a large share of their revenues at certain times of the year. If for some reason they fail to achieve these revenues within these time frames, they have little chance of recouping their losses at other times. I suppose an extreme example of this would be a firm that is engaged solely in the sale of Christmas trees. If sales happen to be down in December, they have no chance of recovering at other times of the year. Think about this as you choose a prospective employer.

- **Supply Chain Issues**

Simply stated, the supply chain represents the flow of materials that are needed to make and deliver finished products. An interruption in the supply chain can prevent a firm from making its own products. Consider the impact on a firm like General Motors if they only had one supplier for steering wheels and a fire destroyed that supplier's factory.

- **Litigation**

Companies that are involved in litigation such as products liability should be examined very closely before accepting a job offer. You may not want to be with a firm facing large-scale litigation, especially if you think they are going to lose the litigation or have to bear huge legal expenses for a sustained period. The funding for large-scale litigation is often obtained at the expense of employees. These include layoffs, salary reductions, hiring freezes and a host of other issues that impact negatively on employees. It's not a pretty scenario for anyone.

- **Reputation**

Some firms have consistently good reputations, others do not. The ones that do usually have managers and employees who are capable and ethical. Simply put, people want to work for them. Check this factor out thoroughly as you consider employment. There are numerous publications available that list the top companies to work for. Stay away from firms that are constantly in the news for ethics violations, criminal conduct, and shoddy management practices. We have all seen far too many of these emerge during the past few years.

You can obtain information on these factors through a combination of your own research and questions you ask during a job interview. We will discuss this topic in more detail later. While some negative information on any firm is almost inevitable, extreme caution should be exercised with regard to joining companies that have negative issues in more than a few of the categories listed above. Remember that you want to do as much as possible to position yourself for success.

If you join a firm that has too many problems, you will in all probability regret the decision sooner or later. Keep in mind that if a firm has had a bad reputation long enough, it probably will not change very soon.

3.   SEARCHING FOR A JOB

In this chapter, we will cover the issues that should be considered in a job search. The objective here is to make sure that you prepare a good resume, utilize job search techniques and resources that are successful, and make maximum utilization of the time you spend searching for a job. The time and effort spent searching for a job may vary greatly from one candidate to the next. These can be due to a variety of factors, some of them as simple as being in the right place at the right time or meeting the right person. For the most part, however, a search that is successful and completed within three to six months will take good planning, preparation and hard work. Let's take a look at some of the things that can help you.

Resume preparation

If you fail to put together a good resume, you will probably not have to worry much about job interviews because employers seldom interview candidates who send them a poorly written or incomplete resume. During my career, I have seen countless resumes from qualified candidates screened out because these individuals simply could not produce their resumes correctly.

The most common reasons for this are:

- The candidate is out of practice. If you have been in your current job for a very long time, you probably have not written a resume in many years, perhaps not at all.
- Sub-standard writing skills. This includes sentence structure, spelling and grammar errors.
- The candidate is not sure what really belongs in a resume.
- Resumes are not focused on relevant facts. They may too long or not well organized. Remember that the definition of the word resume is *"brief" or "short"*
- The resume lacks good physical presentation. It is printed on sub- standard paper, copied on a sub-par copy machine, and in some cases, even hand written!

In order to write a good and effective resume, it is important to put yourself in the shoes of the people who will be reading it. These include Human Resource personnel who conduct initial resume screening, Human Resource executives, the people who will be interviewing you, including your future boss, and possibly others as you move through a typical interview process. Understand that these people have a variety of duties they have to perform and reviewing resumes is only one of these duties. They typically want to spend as little time doing this as possible. This is especially true with Human Resource personnel who may have to screen literally hundreds of resumes a week before forwarding on those that they believe are well qualified for specific jobs. *If your resume gets screened out at this level, the hiring authority will probably never see your resume, regardless of how well qualified you are.* Your chances of getting an interview are slim and none. Should your resume get to the hiring authority, it will then be compared to others that have been forwarded by Human Resources or search firms. Keep in mind that a relatively low percentage of resumes make it this far. When I was in the private sector and needed a management position filled, I would usually ask Human Resources or a search firm to forward me what they considered to be the top fifty resumes. I simply didn't have the time to review any more than that, and I know a lot of my peer group reviewed less resumes than I did.

The typical influx of resumes for a management position was usually 300-400. Therefore, for every job opening, I was seeing under 20% of all resumes received by the company. While a large portion of those screened out were no doubt based on overall qualifications, I am quite sure many were due to poor preparation or appearance.

So, what does a good resume look like? We are going to provide an example, of course, but first let's look at the main attributes of a well prepared resume.

- **Appearance**- Use a good quality paper.
- **Length**- Not more than **two pages long**, perhaps a page and a half if possible.
- **Content**- Because a resume is brief, the content should be well focused to include not only your employment history, but also a list of your areas of expertise and significant achievements in positions you have held. It should also contain sections for education and a brief personal history.
- **Organization**- A methodical and chronological presentation of the content.

The following two pages provide a sample resume. Take a few minutes to review it and then we'll discuss it further. We single spaced the resume which is how you would prepare an actual resume.

Christian Maiale   973-343-7666-Home
2340 N. Weasel Rd.   201-478-1561- Work
Chester, NJ 08076   E Mail: ccm@aol.com

Career law enforcement professional with solid record of achievement as a Special Agent, U.S. Secret Service. Currently Assistant Special Agent in Charge of a large, busy field office. Experience includes managing complex criminal investigations, protection of several U.S. Presidents and other dignitaries, and handling diverse assignments in two dozen foreign countries. Recipient of four Department of the Treasury awards for outstanding service. Specific areas of expertise include:

- ☐ Physical Security   ☐ Executive Protection
- ☐ Computer Security   ☐ Event Security
- ☐ Financial Crimes   ☐ Training

PROFESSIONAL EXPERIENCE

United States Secret Service
Washington, DC

1996-Present
Assistant Special Agent in Charge
Newark NJ Field Office

Tasked with ongoing management of a large field office. The office is staffed by 90 Special Agent and support personnel who conduct investigations of federal crimes such as counterfeiting of US currency, computer related crimes and credit card fraud. Agents also handle the protection of the US President and other dignitaries who visit the Newark district. Accomplishments include:

- Conviction of a group of foreign terrorists who were planning to assassinate a visiting head of state
- Conviction of an eight individuals responsible for the counterfeiting of $12Million in US currency

- Increased office productivity (cases closed) by 15% while maintaining a 99% conviction rate
- Reduced office overtime 18% by modifying scheduling techniques and operating procedures

1991-1996
Assistant Special Agent in Charge
Financial Crimes Division—Washington, DC

Managed a group of eight agents tasked with the oversight of financial crimes handled by Secret Service field offices worldwide. Types of crimes included counterfeiting of US currency, credit card fraud, computer crimes, money laundering, telecommunications fraud, and the forgery of US Savings bonds. Accomplishments included:

- Developed and implemented a computerized case management system now in use by all offices
- Created a global profiling system that led to the conviction of perpetrators in over 200 unsolved cases
- Personally managed global task forces that solved major counterfeiting cases in Asia and the Mid-east
- Led an effort that resulted in the seizure of 2Billion dollars in a money laundering scheme

1987-1991
Special Agent
Office of Training, Washington, DC

Served as an instructor in the Office of Training. Developed and presented course material for basic agents as well as experienced personnel undergoing on the job training. Accomplishments included:

- Developed material for new courses dealing with the investigation of financial crimes
- Introduced and later implemented a plan for a new firearms training course
- Consistently rated at the highest level by students for my preparation and presentation skills

1983-1987
Special Agent
Presidential Protective Division, The White House
Washington, DC

Assigned to the protection detail for President Ronald Reagan. Participated in the protection of the President in the United States and in foreign countries. Planned security for the travel of the President to locations in the United States and abroad. Traveled to all fifty states and eighteen foreign countries. Accomplishments included:

- Managed advance team for the G-7 economic summit in Venice, 1986
- Participated in task force that reviewed and revised White House emergency procedures
- Conducted security arrangements for Camp David Mid–east summit, 1987

1979-1983
Special Agent
Baltimore Field Office, Baltimore, MD

Rose from basic agent to senior agent who handled complex criminal investigations and security advances.

- Earned special achievement award for leading office in arrests, 1981
- Assigned to protective details for three different Presidential candidates during 1980 campaign
- Conducted four month undercover investigation of several organized crime figures

EDUCATION

MA, Criminal Justice, George Washington University, Washington, DC GPA 3.1

BA, Communications, University of Maryland, College Park, MD
- Deans List- four semesters
- Varsity baseball- three years

Attended various Secret Service training courses dealing with a variety of topics

OTHER INFORMATION

Certified as a **Fraud Examiner** by the National Society of Fraud Examiners

Certified as an **Protection Professional (CPP)** by the American Society for Industrial Security

Member of the American Society for Industrial Security and Federal Law Enforcement Officers Association

Outside interests include golf, jogging and gardening

References are available upon request.

The sample resume follows a format that we recommend for our clients. Let's take a look at it one section at a time.

Heading

This should include your name, address, relevant telephone numbers and, if you wish, an e-mail address. Use of an e-mail address is important if you are going to transmit the resume electronically. It also facilitates communication between you and potential employers.

Opening Statement

This is *the most important section* of your resume. It should be designed to get the attention of the reader so that they want to learn more about you. What we recommend here is a brief description of your background and capabilities. It should consist of a narrative of *less than one hundred words* and four to eight bullet points listing your particular areas of expertise. Once the reader has progressed this far, they should have a fairly good idea if your experience and skill set are a match for a certain position. It is important that the narrative portion be well written. You may wish to highlight a few words or phrases to get the reader's attention. The bullet points listing your areas of expertise are important because the reader can readily relate them to job requirements. List areas of expertise that you strongly feel will be of value to a private sector employer. Each of the six points used in the example are relevant skills to most private sector employers who need a security professional. You may also happen to possess skills, such as a Firearms Expert, that simply aren't relevant to most private employers, so leave these out. Concentrate on the skills that are relevant. You can bring up other areas of expertise during an interview, if appropriate. Remember, keep things brief, focused and relevant.

Keep in mind that Human Resource screening personnel and even hiring managers may screen your resume out if your opening statement is poorly written or fails to list relevant skills. They may not even read the rest of the resume. I have seen this occur many times.

Professional Experience

This is the main portion of the resume. Starting with your most recent (or current) position, list your employment dates, position and employment location. Following each employment description, a brief statement of overall duties and responsibilities should follow. The statement should not exceed about 100 words. Following the statement, prepare three to five bullet points that list what you believe are significant achievements. These are important because it gives the reader specifics on your accomplishments. It sets you apart from other candidates who may have less of a track record and gives the employer an indication of what level of performance they can probably expect from you. If you fail to take this approach, the reader may be left with the impression that you do not have significant achievements.

Your professional experience section should cover your entire work history, however, more space should be devoted to what you have done recently than what you may have done many years ago. This is because the reader will invariably have more interest in your more recent work history than what you did early in your career. You can mention jobs that you held more than twenty years ago, but only briefly. Once again, these can be more fully explained in an interview.

Education

In this section, you should list your relevant education, starting with the highest level attained. You should list specific degrees and majors. Grade point averages, if notable, and honors should be listed as should significant extra-curricular activities. I do not recommend listing the year of a degree; it may tend to date you. You can provide this information during an interview, if asked.

You may also want to list other relevant education you have received during your work career. Keep in mind, however, that there are space limitations on a resume.

Other Information

This section should be used to provide any other information you feel is relevant. It can include memberships in professional organizations, professional certifications, and perhaps a few words about your outside interests and hobbies. I do not recommend providing information regarding marital status, children, religious or political affiliation.

Your resume should be printed on good quality paper. You will need some blank sheets of the same paper for cover letters and will also need matching envelopes. In my opinion, it is worth the expense to obtain these items from a printing service rather than to try to do them yourself.

If you feel you need help in preparing your resume, there are a variety of books available in most bookstores. There are also businesses that can provide resume preparation assistance for a fee.

In conclusion, you must dedicate yourself to produce the best resume possible. The ultimate success of your job search depends on it. The number of interviews you generate will depend, to a large extent, on the quality of your resume. Take your time and put in the effort needed to create the best product possible.

Don't be afraid to ask others for copies of their resumes so that you can get some ideas on design, content, presentation and style. The outline we use in our sample has received positive comments from Human Resources and search firm personnel, so we continue to recommend it.

Developing a Job Search

Once you have your resume, you are ready to conduct a job search. This can be a very trying experience, particularly for good jobs that draw a lot of interest. While a search may typically take three to six months, I have seen a lot of people on the job market for up to two years.

The main point to keep in mind is that only about 20-25% of openings for decent jobs are ever placed in the published job market. The remainder wind up in what we call the non-published job market. Let's take a look at examples of each:

Published Market

These are job openings typically placed in newspapers, trade magazines, professional journals and on the internet. If you read these publications, you will find job openings and then follow the instructions on how to apply. You may have already done this.

Non-published Market

These are jobs that never make it into the published market. They usually include jobs that companies place with search firms (headhunters), jobs filled by word of mouth, and positions filled from within an organization.

It's pretty easy to tap into the published job market. If you consistently read want ads and surf the internet, you will come up with most of what is in the published market. While this is relatively easy, it also draws a crowd because everyone in the job market is doing the same thing. As a result, there may be literally hundreds of resumes received for a single opening. The odds of gaining an interview here may be difficult, just based on sheer numbers. Your chances will be slim indeed if you have not written a very good resume. Despite these negatives, this is a basic job search technique that you must utilize on a regular basis. There are internet sites available today that actually gather all the jobs in the published market and put them in one place for you to retrieve. One of the best I have seen for persons in my field is **SMR Group,** which operates out of Washington, DC. They can be found on the internet at **www.securityjobs.net**

The real success in a job search is learning how to find opportunities in the non-published market. While this takes a good bit of time and perseverance, it may present you with the best opportunities and much less competition than published jobs. There are any number of ways to tap into this market and we cannot cover them all. We will however, take a look at some of the most popular and effective methods.

- *Network with people in your industry.* This is the most obvious method of checking out the unpublished market. Start with people you know. Keep track of when you contact them, then re-contact them on a regular basis, perhaps every sixty days. When people you know give you leads, follow up on them as soon as possible. You should also develop a list of people you do not know, but who may be able to assist you. These may include individuals you may have heard of as well as persons whose names you obtained from membership lists of professional organizations.

Make sure you contact people with companies that you know hire on a fairly regular basis.

- *Network with friends and associates.* This method is often overlooked, but can prove to be very effective. These include family members, friends, and others that you may encounter on a regular basis. You never know what job opportunities a person may be aware of unless you ask. One situation I became aware of centered on the owner of a gas station where I took my cars for maintenance. The owner of the station, who was also my neighbor, had a customer who told him that he was out of work and looking for a job in marketing. A few weeks later, the station owner encountered another customer who was in charge of sales and marketing for an area firm. As it turned out, this person was in the middle of hiring marketing personnel for a major expansion. The station owner put his two customers together and the person who was looking for a job was hired within two weeks. I know of yet another case where a person learned of a job opening from his barber, followed up on the lead and wound up getting a six-figure job. Not bad for a few minutes of networking with the barber!

Using Search Firms

As you probably know, many firms do not conduct searches on their own. When they have an opening, particularly for a management position, they use a search firm, often known as a "headhunter" to find candidates for them. The search firm may be on a retainer to the company, hence the name "retained search". At times, the search may be done on a contingent basis, meaning the search firm gets paid only if they find a candidate ultimately hired by their client. The fees charged by search firms vary, but usually wind up being a percentage of the first year salary. Search firms cannot be overlooked as an effective way to tap into the unpublished market. Once these firms have your resume, they will usually enter your name into their database and then review your resume when they have openings in your field.

There are several publications available that list all search firms; both in hard copy and CD-Rom. Once you obtain one of these publications, you can send your resume to as many search firms as you like. When you have done this, you may or may not hear from the firm. They may send you a letter to acknowledge that they received your resume and will contact you if appropriate. You can rest assured, however, that if a job comes along for which you are a good match, you will probably hear from them because they are *paid* to fill vacancies. If you are contacted, you will first be interviewed on the telephone and then possibly in person. Should this go well, you may then be referred to their client for a job interview.

Most search firms will only keep your resume in their database for a year or so. After that, you may have to resubmit a current resume to stay active in their database.

Remember, search firms usually operate on either a retained or contingent basis. On a retained search, the search firm has an exclusive agreement with their client to fill a vacancy. Part of the fee may be paid in advance, the remainder upon filling the position. On a contingent search, the search firm only receives a fee if they are able to fill a position. There may be several search firms trying to fill a position at the same time. Only the one that succeeds receives compensation. Some employers will use firms for contingent searches and still try to fill the position themselves. If they are able to fill it themselves, none of the firms that worked on the search receive any compensation.

In other words, the search firm business can be very competitive, particularly the area of contingent searches.

While most search firms you use will operate on fees paid by employers, some of them receive their fees from the job seeker. These type of firms may want you to pay them several thousand dollars to help you find a job. If you engage one of these firms, be very careful to review any agreements you sign before paying them any money. While some of these firms will guarantee that they will work with you until you find a job, some will just offer you advice and other support services such as resume preparation. If this is the case, make sure that the fee you are paying is worth the service you will receive. A number of job seekers have told me that they have paid these types of firms as much as $10,000; and received little more than advice on how to look for a job and how to write a resume. You can probably get comparable support from reading a few good books written on the subject. Several of my seminar attendees told me that they received more information in the seminar than they did by spending thousands on a fee based search firm.

Networking

While networking was mentioned previously in this section, it is very important and should be expanded upon. Networking is something you should do on a regular basis when searching for a job. Be sure to keep good records of who you talk to, and write yourself a reminder to re-contact them at regular intervals if you feel they may be helpful. A good technique when networking is to ask each person you talk to for the names of *two* other people that you may contact to develop leads. Some people may not be able to give you two other names, but many will. By utilizing this pyramiding technique, you can develop a lengthy list of contacts in a relatively short period of time. You should then refine your list and continue to stay in touch with those who can provide the best potential leads. Establish goals on how many people you will network with in any given week, month, etc. Then do everything possible to meet these goals on a regular basis.

While most networking can be done on the telephone, you may find that from time to time, it is a good idea to meet some of your contacts in person. This is especially true in situations where you feel that a contact has been very helpful to you or may be a good source for future leads. A short office meeting or perhaps a lunch can go a long way toward improving your relationship with selected contacts. Most people will want to help you, but you need to handle your contacts carefully so that you do not become a nuisance.

4. JOB INTERVIEWS

Sometimes job interviews can come easily, very often, they require a lot of time and effort on the part of the job seeker. Whatever the case, the interview represents a crucial part of the job search process. It is an opportunity for both you and a prospective employer to determine if you are right for each other. For that reason, you should spend a considerable amount of time to prepare for an interview. Adequate preparation requires considerable time and attention. In this chapter, we will review a number of items that you should consider in preparing for an interview.

Preparation

Most of the tips provided on preparation are based on common sense. Unfortunately, I have heard of too many stories where failure to follow some basic preparation techniques led to avoidable problems. For that reason, these tips are worth mentioning and include:

- *Research the employer*. You should never go on an interview without getting as much information as you can on the employer's business. This is usually available from annual reports, company web sites, and reports from brokerage firms. Once you have adequate information, you will be in a much better position to determine your potential contribution to the company. You will also be able to better discuss company business with an interviewer.

Things that you should be aware of include company history, senior management, product lines, earnings history, recent company news, and overall reputation. I interviewed a fellow once for a senior position that didn't even know we were a drug company. Such blatant lack of preparation for an interview is almost always a prescription for failure. It certainly was for this fellow.

* *Pick a good time for the interview.* While choosing a time for an interview may be beyond your control, you should try to interview at times where you will be at your best. Interviewing can be a very stressful and time-consuming process. If you are not at your peak, you may well fall short of giving the best account of yourself. I usually tell my clients to get a good night sleep prior to an interview and try to schedule the interview for mid-morning. Mornings are usually better because most of us are more

attentive and possess more energy than perhaps right after lunch or at the end of the day. If however, you are not a morning person, try to steer your interview time to later in the day. If you have to travel out of town to an interview, particularly on an airplane, always try to arrive at your destination the prior evening. I have seen too many job seekers get up at 4am to catch an early morning flight to another city for an afternoon interview. By the time their interview begins, they have been awake perhaps ten hours and have flown several hundred miles. Their clothes may be wrinkled, they are probably tired, perhaps hungry, and they are far from operating at an optimum level. You should avoid this type of scenario if at all possible, even if you have to absorb the cost of a hotel room for one night.

Remember too, your flight may be late and you could miss the interview entirely.

* *Have good directions and arrive on time.* While this is common sense, it often becomes a problem for a variety of reasons. I had a friend who some years ago lined up an interview for a job he had pursued

for almost two years. On the day of the interview, he drove to the interview site, a building in a crowded downtown area of a large city. He wasn't able to park near the building and wound up finding a spot some four blocks away. By the time he found a spot, he only had about five minutes before his interview was scheduled to begin. In addition, it had started to rain hard and he didn't have an umbrella. He literally ran to the building, arriving there ten minutes late, out of breath and soaking wet. The interview didn't go well and he didn't get the job. Unfortunately, sometimes little things do make a difference. Make sure you know how to get to the interview site, and allow enough time to arrive there five to ten minutes early. Don't be afraid to ask the employer about parking and be prepared for things like bad weather and traffic jams. If you do encounter an unavoidable problem getting to an interview, make sure you call the employer.

Appearance

Obviously, we want to look our best for an interview. We all have our own individual tastes for attire, and who is to really say what is the right look for an interview? You may interview with several people and while some may like how you look, others may not. It's hard to say. *That's why we recommend that job seekers present a neutral and neat appearance.* It's the easiest way to pass muster on an interview. After all, you want the interviewer to focus on what you have to say, not what you are wearing. Some tips for a neat and neutral appearance include:

<u>Men</u>

Clean shaven, fresh haircut, beards and moustaches trimmed, fingernails trimmed.

Best to wear a dark suit, white shirt, matching tie, plain socks, plain black or brown shoes that are shined and properly heeled.

Jewelry should be limited to a watch and plain rings. Avoid bracelets, necklaces, gaudy tie tacks, and earrings.

<u>Women</u>

Business attire, neat hairdo, and a limited amount of jewelry. Since I am not an authority on ladies attire, I won't comment any further. I think the point here is made and speaks for itself. Keep it neat and neutral.

Demeanor

The best advice is to be cordial but businesslike. You should not appear to be too stilted or formal, but you also want to avoid too much informality, especially during a first interview. If the interviewer wants to get right down to business, accommodate them and stick to their agenda. If they want to break the ice with some informal conversation, don't be afraid to loosen up a bit. Sometimes, the surroundings in an office may give you a clue about the interviewer. If, for example, you see that the office is filled with golf paraphernalia and you are a golfer, talk a bit about golf if you get the opportunity. But don't bring it up on your own. Let the interviewer take the lead. Also remember to engage in a good firm handshake, maintain eye contact, and keep a nice straight posture. These are all little things, but remember what I said earlier- sometimes little things are important. On a job interview, doing all the little things well may give you an advantage over those who don't do them as well as you.

Questions you will be asked on a job interview and how to prepare for them

While we can't predict exactly what you will be asked on an interview, we have a pretty good idea based on experience. You may not be asked all of these questions, but there is a good chance you will encounter at least some of them. It's best to anticipate these questions in advance and have a good answer rather than be caught off guard and provide a poor or delayed response.

Questions you will probably hear include:

- ***Tell me a little bit about yourself.*** You should anticipate this and be prepared to respond. The best approach to answering this question is to have a prepared response lasting no longer than *90 seconds*. Move quickly through things like where you were born, raised and went to school. Then go into your career in chronological order and talk about the positions you held, what you did and your achievements. At the end mention a few things about outside interests. Remember, you don't have to tell them your age, marital status, religion and other personal information. This is something you should practice before an interview until you are satisfied with content and delivery.

- ***What do you know about our company?*** If you have done your homework, you should be able to easily handle this question. You can gain quite a few points here if you show you had enough interest to conduct some research on the company.

- ***What are a few of your most significant career achievements?*** Expect this one and have a prepared answer. You should be able to discuss three or four items in about two to three minutes. I have seen a number of candidates ill prepared for this question. They have to think long and hard before coming up with an answer. When they do, they realize later that they did not include their best achievements. That's why you want to prepare this answer in advance. A delayed answer here may leave the impression that you lack significant achievements.

- ***I'm sure you've seen the description for this job. How do you feel your background matches up with the job requirements?*** Again, this is one you can prepare for in advance. Review the job requirements thoroughly before the interview, then match them to your skill set and experience. During the interview, recite the main job requirements one at a time and demonstrate to the interviewer how your experience is a match for each particular requirement.

- ***Why do you want to leave your current position?*** This is a question that is almost always asked. Expect it and have a prepared, concise and honest answer. If you are retiring from your current job, the answer is very easy.

- ***What kind of compensation are you looking for?*** I have a belief that he who mentions salary first loses. By mentioning how much money you want, you may be telling the interviewer that you are willing to accept a good bit less than they are willing to pay. This not only undercuts your earnings potential should you take the job, it may also diminish your status as a candidate with the employer. A good answer is "*I'm sure that a company such as yours is willing to pay a salary that is fair and competitive in this industry. By the way, may I ask what the salary range for this job is?* In other words, try to get them to mention salary first. We'll talk more about this issue in the next chapter when we review compensation issues.

- *We have a lot of qualified candidates for this position. Why should we hire you?* The best way to answer this is to remind the interviewer that your past record of success strongly suggests that you will continue to be successful. Also mention again how your background matches up with the job requirements.

- *Where do you see yourself in the next five to ten years?* A good answer for this question is that you would expect your advancement within the company to be commensurate with your achievements and potential. Avoid saying that you would want your managers' job. It's too much of a cliché and can be perceived as threatening.

- *What's the most serious mistake you ever made? How did you learn from it?* This requires a "middle of the road" answer. Discuss something that went wrong, but that you were able to correct rather than something that went awry and may have caused serious consequences.

- ***How do you handle stress and adversity?*** You obviously want to say you handle these issues well. It is best here to give a few examples of how you reacted to these factors successfully in the past.

- ***Explain a serious work related problem you encountered and how you handled it.*** Obviously, you want to be able to talk about something major that you handled well.

- ***What kind of outside interests do you have?*** This can be intended as a probing question to determine how well you may fit in the overall culture of the company. Avoid discussing outside interests that others may feel are controversial.

- ***What kind of performance appraisals have you received in the past few years?*** This is a good question to determine what previous managers have thought of your overall performance and ability. Be prepared to discuss them.

Remember to give full but concise answers. Try not to be too long winded or drift too far away from specific questions. Candidates, in an effort to impress the interviewer, often feel that saying more is better. This is not the case- if you can provide a clear and concise answer to a question, you will make a better impression than if you tend to be too wordy.

Questions you may want to ask on an interview

One of the biggest mistakes made on interviews is failure to ask meaningful questions of the interviewer. **Many candidates ask few if any questions** other than those that relate to compensation. The ability to ask meaningful questions demonstrates preparation, insight, interest and intelligence. These are all critical factors used in evaluating candidates. We recommend preparing questions in advance and writing them down in a notebook that you carry into an interview. When the interviewer provides you with an chance to ask questions, you should indicate that you do have some prepared questions and then ask them, one at a time. Writing them down demonstrates thoroughness and assures that you will not forget to ask questions you deem important. Questions that we feel you should consider asking include:

- ***What do you consider the most important responsibilities of this job?*** This is a very important question because you want to make sure that your impression of major job responsibilities is a close match to that of the hiring manager.

- ***How will my performance be evaluated?*** You should always know the answer to this question. Hopefully, your performance will be evaluated primarily on how well you attained goals and objectives that you and your hiring manager agree on at the start of an evaluation period. We'll talk more about goals and objectives in a later chapter.

- ***What are the characteristics of the person who would be successful on this job?*** You would hope that the answer to this represents a close match to your own characteristics. If it does not, you may not be a good fit for the job.

- **How are important decisions made in this company?** This will give you an idea of how senior management operates and provide some insight on whether the company and their management style is a good fit for you.

- **What is the scope of my authority for budgets, hiring, promotions, discipline, setting goals?** This question is important in determining how much latitude you will have, how closely you will be managed, etc. The answer you get should be important in determining if you want the job.

- **What do you feel are the major challenges of this job during the next five years?** This will help you formulate goals if you take the job. It also may give you a glimpse of where the company is headed, what issues they have on their agenda, and how well they are doing.

- **Why did the previous incumbent leave this job? How long was he/she here?** It's always a good idea to find out why someone left a job that you may want to take. If too many people have held the job over the past several years, it may be a warning sign. The answer you get may even prompt you to contact a past incumbent(s)to get their input.

- *Why did you choose to come to work here? What makes you stay here?* This question will surprise a lot of interviewers. Some of the answers may surprise you. It should, however, give you some information about the company, both positive and negative. If people who impress you have chosen to stay with the company for many years, it makes a strong statement in favor of the company.

- *If I do a good job, what opportunities may be available to me?* It is always good to know if there are opportunities to move ahead and what they may be.

- *What do you think are the major frustrations or obstacles to this job?* This is yet another question that you can use to evaluate if the job is right for you.

- ***How do I compare to other serious candidates?***
  This is a chance to obtain some information on the qualifications of your competition and emphasize that you are the best candidate. You may also learn how many other candidates there are.

Don't be shy about asking as many questions as you may have. Write down the answers and review them after the interview to help you evaluate the company and your potential manager.

Things to avoid during an interview

There have actually been books written on this subject, which strongly suggests that it can be a serious obstacle to interviewing well. While it difficult to anticipate all of the things that should be avoided during an interview, we will examine some of the more common pitfalls. These include:

- Arriving late for an interview or asking to leave before the interview is over.
- Reciting facts to the interviewer that are in direct conflict with your resume.
- Mentioning personal facts or opinions that could jeopardize your candidacy. These include political affiliation, race, religion, marital status, sexual

preference and mistakes in your life that are best left in the past.

- Trying to crush the interviewer's hand with a vice like handshake. A bad idea.

- Encountering a clumsy moment such as spilling coffee or splattering the interviewer with food during a meal. I have seen both happen more than a few times.

- Asking the interviewer questions about their personal lives.

There are obviously many other pitfalls too numerous to cover here. The best advice I can give in this area is to exercise discretion and good common sense at all times.

Second interviews

In most cases, you will have to get through a second interview before you receive a job offer. Very often, two and possibly three candidates may be invited for a second interview. While the hiring manager will probably have an idea of who the leading candidate is, their mind may well be changed by how candidates handle second interviews. Initial interviews usually include a Human Resources executive and the hiring manager, second interviews will often include not only the same individuals, but also an expanded group of people. The expanded group may well include:

- The direct superior of the hiring manager.
- The CEO of the company.
- Peers of the hiring manager. They may interview you individually or as a group.
- Employees who report to your hiring manager (your peers).
- Legal counsel
- An in house or contract psychologist. This is becoming increasingly common.

The main concept to keep in mind when preparing for a second interview is that they are designed to find out which candidate represents the best fit for the organization. The company already feels that you can handle the job or they wouldn't bring you back a second time. Their purpose is to determine how well each candidate fits the corporate culture, how they will probably get along with co-workers, and in the case of the hiring authority, if they want you as a direct report. It is also a second chance for you to see if the company and its workers are a good fit for you.

Once second interviews are concluded, the hiring manager will solicit opinions about you from those who interviewed you. The input received will usually be taken very seriously, particularly input received from senior management. At the end of this process, a decision will be made regarding who is the top candidate and whether to put together an offer. Other candidates may be dropped from consideration. Sometimes, all candidates are dropped from consideration and the company may start a new search.

Some tips for second interviews include:

- Be prepared for a long day. You may have to meet with several people and one of the meetings may include a meal. This means that you are going to have to stay alert and at peak performance for an extended period of time. The process may even include an invitation for you and your spouse to have dinner with the hiring manager. Consider this yet another interview, but, if you reach this point, you are probably the leading candidate.

- Re-emphasize the points you made during your initial interview. Talk about what you can do for the company and don't be shy about asking questions.

Do not be concerned about asking some of same questions you asked during the first interview. **Do be concerned**, however, if you get different answers. Be sure to ask where the company is in the hiring process and when they plan to make a decision.

- Try to stay relaxed and avoid being overly stiff or formal. The interviewers would rather see you as you really are on a day to day basis.

- If at the end of the process you feel you want the position, **ask if you can have the job**. This demonstrates interest and enthusiasm. While you may not get an immediate answer, you may be able to determine if you are the top candidate and that an offer is in the works.

- After the interviews, drop short thank you notes or e-mail to the persons you met and mention that you would look forward to working with them.

- If you haven't heard anything from the company after about two weeks, follow up with a telephone call.

5.   COMPENSATION ISSUES

In this chapter, we will discuss the issue of compensation. After all, compensation is the main reason most of us work. Unfortunately, most persons coming out of the public sector are not familiar with private sector compensation issues. This lack of familiarity can lead to under pricing yourself when you take a job. **Remember that if you take a job at less than market, you will never recover that money.** As an example, let us say you are completing a 25-year public sector career at a salary of $60,000 and your retirement pay will be $35,000 a year. You are offered a private sector job at $50,000. When you combine this with your retirement pay, you will now make $85,000 a year; a good bit more than you earned working in the public sector. This sounds like a good situation, after all, you are now going to make 40% more than you earned when you received only a public sector income.

Let's suppose, however, that your private sector job would have paid $70,000 a year had you handled your salary negotiation a little better? Let's also assume that you plan to work in the private sector job for 15 years. Over a fifteen-year period, that $10,000 a year difference comes to

$150,000, quite a bit of money that you will probably never see. Money left on the table when you accept a job offer is usually never made up to you by the employer. They may like your work and promote you, but they are never going to tell you they hired you cheap and pay you the money you could have had if you had negotiated a better starting salary.

In addition to base salary, there are quite a few other compensation issues that most public servants have not experienced in their careers. These include signing bonuses, stock options, deferred compensation, 401K plans and lump sum retirements. There are also private sector fringe benefits that are not found in the public sector which have significant value. You should find out about all of these things in the pre-employment process.

Gaining some familiarity with these issues prior to entering the private sector will give you a better chance of achieving compensation consistent with your private sector peer group. After all, you want to earn as much as you can. If you are like most career public servants, you have not accumulated a lot of wealth in your career. A private sector career of perhaps ten to twenty years will give you a chance to do that, provided that you maximize the opportunity.

Always keep in mind that your services are *for sale*, they are not *on sale*.

Let's now examine various compensation issues mentioned above.

Benchmarking of salaries

Private sector salary levels are not pulled out of thin air (most of the time). They are developed by Human Resource personnel using a variety of factors. These include:

- Geographic location. The cost of living varies widely around the country.
- Level of expertise, education and training needed to do the job
- Supply and demand (how hard is it to attract qualified employees to the company and the area)
- Level of responsibility and authority the job has in the organization

Most firms will take these factors (and others) and use them to "level" a job. That means they will compare the importance of the job to others in their organization and come up with a salary range they feel the job warrants. They will then compare their finding to what other companies pay for the same position. This information is available from a variety of data bases, including one known as SIRS (Salary Information Retrieval System). Once they have all of this information, they will place the position into a pay grade or range, much the same as government agencies and the military. Pay grades have ranges, the higher the pay grade the higher the salary range.

Let's take a look at how all of this may work in a real situation:

Suppose that an engineering executive has an approved budget that calls for creating a new position to hire a mid-level engineer. He prepares a job description and forwards it to Human Resources. Human Resources levels the job and finds that is worth about $80,000 a year. SIRS data shows that similar jobs in the same industry and same geographic area are compensated in a range between $70,000 and $95,000 per year. The mid point between the low and high of this range is $82,500. The company now knows that in order to pay the mid point for this job in their industry, they will need to pay around $82,500. If they want to attract better candidates, they may need to offer a salary closer to $90,000.

Now let's say that the mid management level pay grades in the company are as follows:

Level 1	$50,000 to $70,000 a year
Level 2	$60,000 to $80,000 a year
Level 3	$70,000 to $90,000 a year
Level 4	$80,000 to $100,000 a year
Level 5	$90,000 to $110,000 a year

Notice that the pay grades have pretty wide ranges and contain some overlap. This is not unusual.

In the above example, the job will be placed into either a Level 3 or 4 pay grade. Let's say it is placed into Level 3 since that will enable the company to make an offer consistent with the salaries being offered for similar positions in their industry. This means that the company has the latitude to fill the job anywhere between $70,000 and $90,000 a year. Most companies expect to fill a job at the mid point of a salary range (in this case that will be about $80,000) but if they can, they may hire closer to the bottom of the range. You of course, should want to be hired closer to the top of the range, but you probably don't even know what the range is for the job. Remember, that if you take this job at $72,000 rather than let's say, $82,000 a year, you will forego $10,000 a year in salary for *each* year you work for the company. If you are coming from a government job that paid you $80,000 a year and are going to receive a yearly pension of $40,000, a salary of $70,000 in this case may leave you more than happy. But suppose you could have gotten $80,000 or even $85,000? Let's look at a few ways that you may be able to do just that.

How to avoid under pricing yourself

A former boss of mine, who was Vice President of Human Resources for a very large firm, had a theory about salary negotiations that I believe is very important:

"He who mentions salary first loses"

It is not uncommon for hiring manager to ask a candidate how much money they will need to accept a position. How you handle that question is very important in determining whether or not you under price yourself or not. Let's take the example I used above. If the candidate answers that he is looking for about $70,000, that's probably what he will receive. If he says $80,000, there is a good chance that he will receive that, since it is at the midpoint of the salary range. You might even get close to $90,000 if the employer thinks you are a particularly good candidate. If you ask for $65,000, you will probably be offered $70,000 and think your boss is a really nice fellow who took good care of you. Remember, they can't pay less than $70,000 because that is the minimum of the pay grade. If you ask for less than $60,000, the manager may think you are not skilled enough to fill the job. And if you ask for more than $90,000, you could jeopardize your candidacy because your request exceeds the maximum amount for the pay grade.

Given these factors, how do you handle this type of question?. There are a few things you can do.

One tactic that I have found works very well is to answer the question with:

"I am somewhat flexible on salary. I'm sure that a company of your caliber and reputation will compensate this position in a manner consistent with your industry and other positions in this company. By the way, may I ask what the salary range is for this position?

You should be able to get an answer to this question. If you do, you will learn that the pay range for the job used in the example is between $70,000 and $90,000 a year. Armed with this information, you can now easily ask for between $80,000 and $82,000, knowing that this is the mid point for the range and knowing that most firms have little problem filling a position at a range mid point. If you feel you are an exceptionally strong candidate and want to be a little aggressive, you can even go higher. If your salary expectations are considerably higher than the maximum of the range, you may feel that you no longer wish to remain a candidate unless the employer is willing to put the job in a higher salary grade. They probably won't, but it doesn't hurt to ask.

Another thing you can and should do is to conduct your own research on what a particular job pays. This should be done before you even reach the salary negotiation stage. You can do this by calling on contacts you may have in your field that work for other companies. This should give you a pretty good idea of the compensation level for a similar job. You may even be able to reach out to a contact that has access to SIRS data in your area or pay to get the data yourself.

Under pricing is a particularly serious problem with persons entering the private sector for the first time. Sometimes, it can also be an issue for those who are already in the private sector because they fail to utilize a few techniques that can give them an advantage. Don't be one of them.

Bonuses, salary increases, and stock options

There are other types of compensation that are common in the private sector and do not exist in public service. Bonuses are not available to the majority of public sector employees and stock options are not available at all. Both of these represent significant income potential and should be understood before entering into the salary negotiation stage.

- *Bonuses.* Many private sector jobs are eligible for bonuses. The two main types of bonuses I have encountered are *signing bonuses and performance bonuses. Signing bonuses* are given at the start of employment as an extra inducement for the candidate to join a firm. They can range from a few thousand dollars to a percentage of your starting base salary. While some firms will tell you that the job includes a signing bonus, many will not divulge this unless you ask. If an employer does not raise the issue of a signing bonus, you should bring it up yourself. The worst that can happen is you are told there is no signing bonus with the job. If you don't at least ask, you may well leave money on the table that could have easily been yours.

Performance bonuses, by definition, are tied into how well you do your job and how well the company does during any given time frame, usually a calendar year. They are usually a percentage of salary and can range from as low as 5% of base salary to as much as 100% of salary for senior positions. No firm is going to be able to promise you a pre-determined performance bonus for each year. Obviously, your performance and the overall profitability of the company year to year are the main factors that drive this issue. You should, however, during salary negotiations, determine if your position will be eligible for performance bonuses. If so, what will the average percentage be if you do a good job and the company posts good results? This will give you a pretty good idea of what you should be able to look forward to in addition to your base salary. Always keep in mind, however, that a bonus is never guaranteed and it can be impacted by many factors. Most of the time, though, your bonus will increase with your length of employment. If you start a job with a bonus equal to 10% of your base, that percentage will probably increase, along with your base salary, as you complete additional years of service.

- *Salary increases.* You should ask how often base salaries are reviewed and eligible for increase. Normally, salaries are reviewed at least once a year and are eligible for increase based on a number of factors such as job performance and inflation. While such increases are by no means automatic, they are usually granted to all employees who are performing at an acceptable level. They typically range from 3-6%, a little higher in some cases.

- *Stock options.* Stock options, as you will see, can add significantly to your compensation, in some cases they can make you wealthy. They can also fail to add to your compensation at all. It all depends on how many shares of options you receive and how well your company stock does over a period of time.

Most public servants may have heard of stock options, but few understand what they really are. They are, by definition, an option given to an employee by a publicly held company that entitles the employee to purchase the stock of the company at a certain price for a specified period of time, usually up to ten years. When an option is granted, it is at a certain price, known as the *exercise price.* This is usually the price that the company stock is selling for on the open market at the time the option is granted to the employee.

Once an option is granted, there is usually a waiting period of one year before the employee can actually exercise the option. Once the year has passed, the employee can exercise the option any time until the option period (usually ten years) expires. **Exercising the option simply means that**

you are buying the stock at the exercise price.
You can then hold onto the stock for as long as you
want or sell it on the open market, usually through a
broker. When you do sell the stock, the difference
between the exercise price and market price is your
profit. Let's examine an example:

Suppose that on 10/1/2001, the ABC Company
grants John Smith a stock option of 1000 shares of
company stock. The exercise price is $20 a share,
which is what the stock is selling for on the open
market at the time of the grant. The option expires
worthless on 10/1/2011. On 6/12/05, Smith notices
the stock of the ABC company is selling on the
open market for $35 a share. Smith decides that he
needs some money to remodel his home and wants
to use his gain from the option grant. So he
exercises his option, meaning he buys 1000 shares
of his company stock from his company at $20 a
share, which is the exercise price. His total cost is
$20,000. He then sells the 1000 shares of stock
through his broker. The difference between the
exercise price and sale price is $15 a share, so in
this case Smith will realize a profit of $15,000. He

will have to pay ordinary income tax on the gain at whatever tax rates apply in his income bracket. Usually you can buy and sell the stock on the same day.

If Smith exercised the option(bought the stock) and held it for more than one year before selling it, he would still have to pay tax, but at a capital gain rate of 20%, which, in all probability, is lower than the rate in his regular tax bracket.

Remember that stock options have unlimited upside but really no downside except for taxes. The worst that could have happened to Smith is that his company stock never went up or even went down during the option period. In this case, he would not have exercised because there was no money to be made. However, he does not lose any money, the option simply expires worthless. **So, don't ever reject an option grant. Believe it or not, I have seem people do just that.**

During a salary negotiation, you should determine if the position will entitle you to regular stock option grants. Some firms will even use options as part of a signing bonus. Option income can represent a significant boost to your overall compensation, particularly if your firm does well over a period of time. There are countless stories of mid level employees in firms such as **Microsoft** who became millionaires from stock options because they were in the right place at the right time. While it may be a stretch to imagine this happening to you, you just never know. It is not uncommon over a career to realize significant gains from option income. It happened to me and many others that I know. You just have to be in the right place at the right time.

If your position is eligible for options, you will probably receive them at regular intervals, possibly every year or two. The number of shares received is usually tied into a formula that takes into consideration factors such as base salary, your pay grade, performance appraisals, and length of time with the company. The number of shares received should increase with your length of service and promotions.

Private sector benefits.

There are a number of other benefits found in the private sector that you should become aware of during the interview process. These include:

- *401K Plans.* While 401K plans were rare as recently as twenty years ago, they are now found in most private sector jobs. In most cases, these plans allow you to save, on a tax-deferred basis, a portion of your salary. Your employer may then match your contribution up to a certain amount. Let us say I am earning $6000 a month in gross salary and I can contribute up to 6% of that to my 401K plan. My employer then provides a 50% match to my contribution. I am saving, on a tax deferred basis, $360 a month and my employer is kicking in an extra $180 month for a total contribution of $540 a month. I then invest this money in a variety of investment vehicles made available by the plan. All contributions and subsequent earnings accumulate tax free until I withdraw money from the plan. Hopefully, you will not have to do this until after retirement. If you want to know more about 401K plans, there is plenty of material available from your broker, on the internet, and in most bookstores.

- *Pension Plans*. Most private sector firms have a pension plan. These plans will pay you a monthly annuity or a lump sum benefit when you reach retirement age. You will usually have to be employed by a firm for a period of anywhere from five to ten years to become eligible for benefits. These plans, depending of how they are structured, can represent a significant portion of your retirement income. They are separate and distinct from 401K plans. The amount of the benefit you receive may be reduced by what you receive in social security benefits and public sector retirement annuities.

- *Medical Benefits*. These are often more comprehensive than those found in the public sector and may be provided at no expense to you. In many companies, however, the employee has to pay part of the premium. You may elect not to do this if your public sector retirement benefit includes health insurance.

- *Other common benefits include:*

• *Tuition refund*	• *Paid vacations and sick leave*
• *Discounts in the company store*	• *Relocation benefits*
• *Disability Insurance*	• *Leave for jury or military duty*
• *Life Insurance*	• *Company car*
• *Paid Family Leave*	

Find out as much as you can about company benefits and use them to the fullest extent possible.

If the company offers benefits that you do not need, such as medical benefits, ask if they will offer you extra compensation in lieu of the benefits. Some firms offer this type of flexibility, others will not. But is doesn't hurt to ask.

6.   MAKING THE TRANSITION

Starting a new job always presents its share of problems. If you have never worked in the private sector, the number of issues you encounter will be even greater than normal. This is particularly true during the first six months to one year in a new job. In this chapter, we will take a look at several of these issues and how to best deal with them.

Handling a job offer

If you go through the entire interview process and emerge as the leading candidate, you will probably receive a job offer. The offer may be presented verbally or in writing. If you find the offer satisfactory and want to join the company, you will want to accept the offer. If the offer does not meet your overall requirements, you can try to negotiate a better package for yourself. Once you are satisfied with an offer, you should ask that it be put in writing and sent to you. You should then accept the offer with a return registered letter, even if you already gave a verbal acceptance. Most firms will provide you with a written offer as a matter of procedure. The offer letter should include the position title, all details of your compensation, and a start date. Written offers and acceptances protect both the employer and employee and should be maintained by both parties on a permanent basis.

Establishing goals and objectives

Once you start a new job, you will want to establish goals and objectives. To an extent, this may already be done for you by your manager or through a job description that you are given. In other cases, it may be up to you to establish these on your own or at least provide significant input. As a new employee, you really can't determine goals and objectives until you learn more about your job and the company. While you may inherit some ongoing projects and problems that need resolution, you will eventually develop long range strategies that will contribute to the success of your employer.

The best approach is to set **initially only short-term goals**. These goals, which should be achieved during the first three to six months, should be geared to learn about the company and how your function fits into the overall business plan. This will enable you to eventually establish longer-term goals.

Short term goals may include but are not limited to:

- Learning about the history of the company and its product lines or services.

- Meeting with your peers to get their input on what they feel are the important elements of your job. In other words, how do they see your job fitting into the big picture?

- Visit key company locations, particularly those that impact most on your duties and responsibilities. Meet the management at these locations.

- Meet with senior management to get their input on how they feel your function can best contribute to the success of the organization.

- Stay in regular contact with your manager to obtain feedback on what you are accomplishing during the orientation period.

- Begin to formulate your own impressions for specific long terms goals and objectives. Discuss these with your manager.

At the conclusion of your initial three to six month period, you should be ready to establish long term goals. The goals should be discussed with your manager, agreed to, and put in writing for later review. Be sure to give your manager a copy. As you develop long term goals, keep the following in mind:

- Do not establish goals you cannot meet. It is best to work within a plan that sets forth a reasonable number of key goals that can be attained during a given time frame. Most companies require personnel to prepare goals and objectives on a yearly basis.
- Prepare goals where attainment can be measured objectively. If, for example, one of your goals is to reduce overhead in your department by 10%, state that specifically in your goals. That number can then be measured against actual results. If you simply state that you will reduce overhead, you won't know if you achieved the goal to the satisfaction of your manager. You may reduce the overhead 10% and think you did a good job, your manager, on the other hand, may feel you should have achieved a 20% reduction.

Here are a few examples of vague goals and objectives that should be avoided:

- Conduct physical security surveys of key overseas locations.
- Reduce overtime hours in the guard force.
- Develop and implement key loss prevention programs.

Here are the same goals written in an objective and *measured* manner:

- Conduct physical security surveys at *six* locations in Europe and South America.
- Reduce overtime hours in the guard force by *10%* through flextime schedules.
- Develop and implement loss prevention programs in the areas of *Information Protection and Employee theft.*

If you prepare your goals as written above, it will be relatively easy for you and your manager to determine if you achieved them. How well you did them is another issue.

The progress of goals should be reviewed on a regular basis to make sure you are on track. If, for example, you set a goal to visit six company locations during a specific calendar year and you haven't visited any by September, it may be time to get started.

It is also important to realize that goals are not necessarily cut in stone. Circumstances may arise that will cause you to add or delete certain goals from your agenda. You may be planning to spend a good bit of time on a project that is delayed or cancelled. Conversely, you may encounter a situation that was not present at the time you initially established goals. When this occurs, make sure you adjust your written goals accordingly and advise your manager in writing. At the end of your evaluation period, you want to make sure that both you and your manager are operating from the same set of goals and objectives. I once had a subordinate that set a key objective involving security integration of a large construction project. He expected that this task would take up about 20% of his time during the next year and for this reason, had this listed as a main objective for that year. Shortly into the year, senior management canceled the project. Instead of adjusting his goals and objectives, this person left them as written. When he and I reviewed the progress of his goals at the mid year, he was hard pressed to explain what he had done with all of the time he was going to spend on the cancelled project. It is difficult to evaluate performance when something like this occurs. It places both the employee and manager in a difficult position. That's why it is important to regularly review progress made in attaining goals and make adjustments when necessary. It will keep you and your manager on the same page and enable your performance to be evaluated in a fair and objective manner.

Always keep in mind that if you and your manager agree on a written set of goals and you consistently achieve those goals, you will in all probability enjoy long term success in your position.

Becoming part of the corporate culture

The ability to learn and fit into a corporate culture is often as important as how well you do a job. There are many examples available of persons who were able to get the job done, but simply were not a good fit for the company or the job. When this happens, both the company and employee often wind up unhappy.

While it is difficult to determine a company's culture during the pre-employment process, you will usually have a pretty fair idea once you have been on the job for six months to one year. During this time, you will talk to enough people and make enough observations to give you a pretty good idea of how the company and its employees operate and interact. While most companies share many common cultural attributes, they all differ in some ways.

Some differ dramatically, depending on industry type, company size, style of senior management, level of profitability, and types of employees. While the number of culture characteristics can be endless and vary in importance, there are some that a new employee should learn as soon as possible. A few of these include:

- *Management Style.* This can range from a very authoritarian to a participatory style. In some companies, decisions are made by senior management and handed down for implementation. There are few, if any consultations with subordinates. In other firms, senior management will consult extensively with subordinates in developing strategies and making decisions. It is important to determine management style and adapt to it as soon as possible, even if it is different from what you experienced in your previous career.

- *Off the job activities.* Some companies are very focused on non-work activities such as athletic leagues and social functions. These activities can be formalized and maintained by the company or organized on an informal basis by employees. I once had a boss who liked to have lunch with his staff every Friday. The lunches seldom involved business, they were strictly social. He also liked to take his staff to athletic events from time to time. I found over a period of many years that those of us who participated in these activities got along much better with this fellow on the job. That may not have been fair to those who chose not to participate, but that's the way it was in this case. Participation in these types of activities is usually a personal choice. You may not have the time or inclination to participate. If after hours activities are an important element of the corporate culture, you may find that some participation contributes to your overall success and satisfaction on the job.

How success will be measured

It can be very difficult at times to determine how an organization or a particular manager measures success. Public agencies are service oriented, corporations, for the most part, exist solely to generate a profit. There are, however, certain key characteristics of a successful person regardless of organization. These include:

- *Meeting measurable goals.* As mentioned previously, you should attempt to set goals that are measurable because it is relatively easy to determine if the goals have been met. If, for example, you set a beginning of the year goal to reduce overhead 12% and achieve that objective, you have achieved what you set out to do. Managers, for the most part, appreciate the efforts of employees that consistently achieve goals. It is a key element of success.

- *Handling unusual incidents well.* Most employees handle routine tasks well, but those who perform well in a crisis or under unusual circumstances will stand out and gain management recognition. Most employees view these circumstances as burdensome or foreboding, the successful person sees them as challenge and opportunity.

- *Getting along with all levels of employees.* Regardless of how well you do your job, it is very important to get along with your co-workers, regardless of their position. While it may be difficult, if not impossible to get along with everyone, acquiring a reputation as a person who is friendly, fair and approachable can often be as important as how you actually do your job. There are many individuals in organizations that consistently achieve high levels of performance, but fail to get ahead due to their interpersonal skills.

- *Increasing the demand for your services.* When persons in an organization notice that an individual does a good job and can add value, they usually will seek out that person when they need something done. As the demand for your services, increases, so does your value. It is an important element to success.

Why some of us fail

While most will do well in a second career, some will ultimately fail to achieve success. In some cases, the lack of success may be purely circumstantial; they may encounter a reduction in force, the company may be sold, or they may encounter a difficult manager. Notwithstanding these circumstances, some will fail due to issues that are well within their ability to control. These include, but are not limited to:

- *Lack of drive and initiative.* Some who enter second careers (as well as many in their initial careers) consistently fail to maintain sufficient drive and initiative to get the job done. This is usually noticed rather quickly and can lead to a very brief tenure with an organization. This is especially true in our current corporate environment.

- *Unwillingness to learn.* A fair number of persons don't want to learn new skills and keep up with technology, particularly in the later stages of their careers. This can often be a prescription for failure, particularly in the current business climate. I once had an employee in his second career that refused to learn basic computer skills, such as e-mail and using internet search engines. He said he only had a few years until retirement and had no interest in this area. This type of an attitude is not what employers are looking for and it is usually not tolerated for very long.

- *Using bad judgment.* While we all sometimes fail to exercise the best judgment, those who consistently fail to exercise good judgment in work situations will fail. This is especially true if such failure causes the organization a serious financial loss, legal exposure, or harm to their reputation. Keep in mind that actions which may be correct and appropriate in a law enforcement or military scenario may be totally inappropriate in a corporate setting.

- *Not measuring up to your peer group.* Many managers tend to compare their subordinates to each other in terms of overall job performance. Those who consistently fail to achieve the same performance levels as their peer group are often expendable, particularly if the organization experiences a downsizing. I recently finished a consulting assignment for a very large, multinational firm. It has been their practice for years to evaluate their employees yearly and assign them a numerical rating that places them between the 1st and 99th percentile in the organization. If you received a rating of 6, for example, you were rated among the top 6% of employees, a 93 placed you in the bottom 7 %. If an employee winds up in the bottom 10% two years in a row, they usually face termination. Each year the process starts anew. The company constantly seeks to eliminate the weakest links in the chain.

FOLLOW UP AND QUESTIONS

We sincerely hope that this book benefits you as you plan and embark on your career path. The book should provide useful information as you move through the various stages of your transition. It should also serve as a handy reference once you accept and start a new job.

If you have any questions regarding what is covered in this book, or would like to have our individual support as you search for a job, give us a call or send an e-mail. We also provide the material shown in this book as a comprehensive, interactive one-day seminar for groups of 15 or more. Call us for details and cost estimates.

Michael V. Maddaloni, President
BUSINESS SECURITY SOLUTIONS, INC.
Phone: 843-681-9742
Fax: 843-681-8321
E-Mail: bussecsol@aol.com

Joanne Brennan, President
SECURITY JOBS NETWORK, INC.
Phone: 866-767-5627
Fax: 703-995-4343
http://www.securityjobs.net
jbrennan@securityjobs.net

Jerry Brennan, President

SECURITY MANAGEMENT RESOURCES, INC

Global Executive Search Consultants

Phone: 540-428-2020

http://www.smrgroup.org

E-Mail: jerry.brennan@smrgroup.org

ABOUT THE AUTHOR

Mike Maddaloni, a native of Philadelphia, Pennsylvania, holds a BS in Management from La Salle University.

In 1972, Mike was commissioned as a Special Agent with the U.S. Secret Service. His career included six years as a field agent investigating crimes against the U.S. Treasury. He then served four years with the Secret Service White House Detail, where he conducted domestic and foreign security advances for both Presidents Carter and Reagan. During his career, Mike earned three Department of the Treasury Special Achievement Awards.

In 1982, Mike joined Wyeth Pharmaceuticals as Director of Security, where he was responsible for worldwide security and loss prevention programs. In 1991, he was promoted to Assistant Vice President of Worldwide Security. During his career in the private sector, Mike developed comprehensive security programs in areas that included protection of information, security for travel and special events, executive protection, crisis management, pre-employment screening, and asset protection. He handled several high profile investigations concerning theft of trade secrets, extortion, and product tampering. Mike also developed loss prevention strategies that significantly reduced company exposure to product diversion schemes and internal fraud.

In 1996, Mike formed Business Security Solutions, Inc. a security consulting firm which specializes in corporate security issues and the protection of high profile clients. He also provides transition training and support for law enforcement and military personnel who plan to move into private sector careers. During his career, Mike has worked in all fifty states and in more than thirty foreign countries.

Mike has spoken extensively on corporate security issues and has appeared on several televised talk shows to discuss a variety of security topics.

He is designated as both a certified protection professional and a certified fraud examiner. Mike maintains residences in Hilton Head, South Carolina and Philadelphia.